#LifeHacks for HAPPINESS

KIM HANKINSON

This book belongs to:

....

Age: ....

The best thing about me: ....

....

My lovely face!

For all those little lions with a small voice
but a big heart. Let's hear you roar!

– Kim

Published by b small publishing ltd.
www.bsmall.co.uk

Text and illustrations copyright © b small publishing ltd. 2023

1 2 3 4 5   ISBN 978-1-913918-59-0

Text, Design and Illustrations by Kim Hankinson
Editorial by Sam Hutchinson. Cover design by Vicky Barker.

Printed in Lithuania on FSC-certified paper from well-managed forests
and responsible sources.

British Library Cataloguing-in-Publication Data. A catalogue record for this book is available
from the British Library.

HOW TO
USE THIS BOOK

This book is full of daring-dreaming-discovering activities everyone can try. Starting on any page, do as many activities as you can fit into a day and in any order you like.

The activities are colour-coded. Match the activity key on page 4 with the coloured circles by each activity in the contents list to help you choose what sort of activity you would like to do. There are extra pages for notes and doodles too.

Have fun exploring your wonderful world with a little more confidence and kindness!

CONTENTS CHECKLIST:

Who says a leopard can't change its spots?
Give this leopard a bold new look.

ACTIVITY KEY

EXPLORE	DARE	MOVE	CREATE	SKILLS	CAREFUL!	HELP	BODY

Always ask an adult when you see a red warning symbol.

Super STAR

Did you know that we are made from the same ingredients as stars? Copy out these stars and decorate your room with them to remind yourself daily that you are an interstellar wonder!

DAILY DARE

Choose your favourite from the two options as fast as you can! Try this game with friends and family.

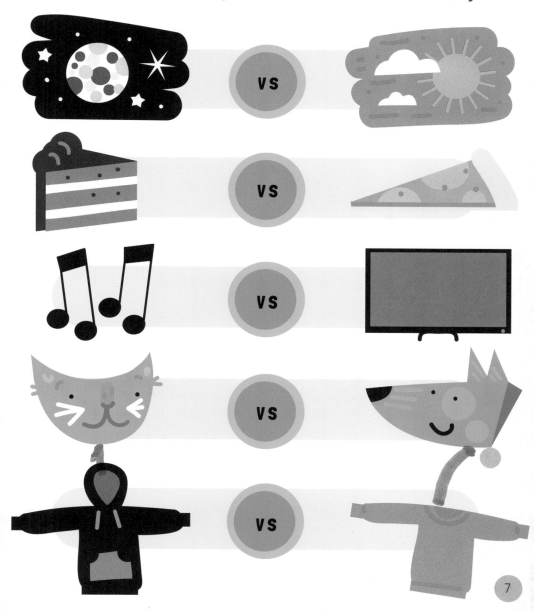

Best friend

Be your own best friend! Write a nice letter to yourself with sentences that start with ...

 ★ **I LIKE THAT YOU ARE ...**

 ★ **YOUR BEST FEATURE IS YOUR ...**

 ★ **YOU ARE GOOD AT ...**

 ★ **MY FAVOURITE PART OF YOUR PERSONALITY IS ...**

 ★ **YOU'RE FUNNY WHEN ...**

 ★ **YOU ARE NICE BECAUSE ...**

If you want, try writing to other friends first for practice. You might have days when you don't feel the bee's knees, but being kind to yourself (and others too) can really make a difference!

DAILY DARE

Smile at as many people as you can
and count how many smile back.

Be a cheerleader

Support someone or something you care about.
Get up and cheer them along!

Eye-eye captain

Have a staring competition!

Face a friend with your eyes shut. On the count of three, open your eyes. The game is to make eye contact for as long as you can, and the first one to look away loses. No blinking now!

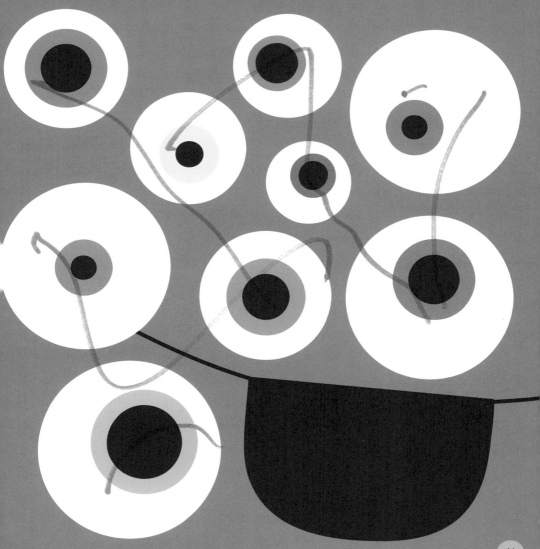

Make a stand!

Practise these confidence exercises
so that you are ready for action!
All standing poses start with 'posture power'.

POSTURE POWER
Standing tall is a great
way to feel big! Lift the
top of the head as if
it's pulled by an invisible
string. Let the shoulders
fall down and back.

Pull your tummy muscles in
towards your back without
arching over... and breathe!

POWER SQUATS
Plant your feet. Squat your
bottom down and up as if
trying to sit on an invisible
chair. Keep your back
straight. Don't lean the knees
over the toes or lift your
heels from the floor.

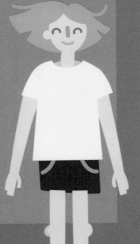

SPRING-INTO-
ACTION JUMPS

Get those energy levels
up. If you're feeling a little
shy or nervous, jump up
and down 20 times, keeping
your body nice and loose!

Breathe and stay comfortable. It should feel good, not a strain.

BE A WARRIOR!

From power posture, turn one foot all the way to the side. Turn the other diagonally to point nearly in the same direction. Next, reach your arms out. Turn to face the foot pointing to the side and then take a big step into a lunge! Your knee should not lean over your ankle. After counting to 20, repeat on the other side.

ARM-STRENGTHENING AIR PUNCH

Get your arm ready for getting noticed and cheering along! Stretch one arm out and punch the air above your head ten times. Repeat with the other arm. Don't go too fast.

... AND, RELAX!

BREATHE DEEP

Lay on the floor and slow your breathing. When you breathe in your belly should rise, and when breathing out it should fall.

Up start!

Use the steps to plan a challenge. The sky's the limit!

When you've filled in the mountain scene as instructed below, you'll start at the bottom and start climbing your challenge mountain!

GOAL

Find your goal? It can be anything, from running a lap in a certain time to perfecting an underwater handstand.

COMPLETE BY

When do you need to complete your challenge by? Choose a deadline even if you don't need one as it's sometimes helpful to have a goal. Base it on how long the next steps will take.

HOW

Research in books, listen to podcasts and go online to learn about people who've achieved your goal and how they did it. There may even be local clubs you can join.

FIRST STEP

These small but important beginnings will get you to the next level. Things like gathering equipment, creating a schedule and learning basic skills. If you need to finish something else before you start, write that here too.

GOAL:

....

....

COMPLETE BY:

HOW:

....

....

....

....

....

FIRST STEPS:

....

....

....

DAILY DARE

Dance like no one's watching
(then do it when they are).

Inspiration station

Collect together images of people you admire and words you think are positively powerful, and make your own collage artwork for your wall.

Sometimes this art will inspire and sometimes it will uplift you, but remember not to compare yourself negatively. You are the most wonderful version of you possible, and there is only one of you in the whole world!

You're blowing up!

You are spectacular! Write out your
name and decorate it in your own style!

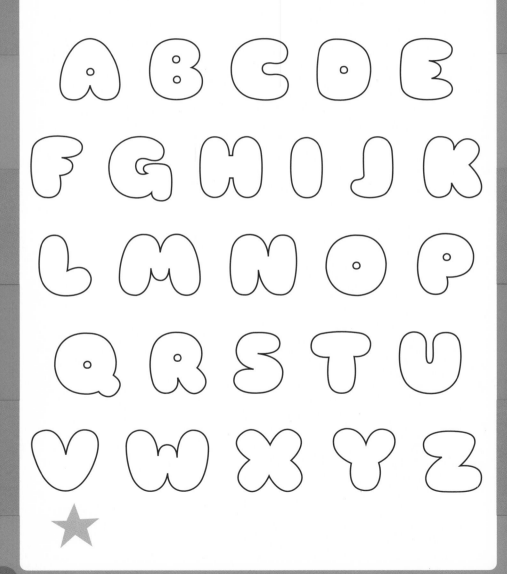

I like to move it!

Exercise can make you feel strong AND it releases happy chemicals in the brain too!

Here are a few sports you could try. There are hundreds of ways to enjoy moving about, you just need to find something YOU like!

MARTIAL ARTS

GYMNASTICS

DANCE!

TENNIS AND BADMINTON

SWIMMING

RUNNING

TRAMPOLINE

ORIENTEERING

CYCLING

SKATEBOARDING

VOLLEYBALL

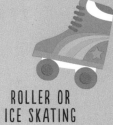

ROLLER OR
ICE SKATING

SKIING

YOGA

CLIMBING AND
BOULDERING

SURFING AND
PADDLEBOARDING

WATER
SPORTS

CIRCUS
SKILLS

GOLF

HORSE RIDING

TEAM SPORTS
(There are LOTS!)

Yes chef!

Start your day off right! Eat a yummy pancake breakfast and learn a new recipe too.

You will need

1 TEASPOON BAKING POWDER
3 BIG SPOONS OF YOGHURT
100 GRAMS FLOUR
3 EGGS
BUTTER FOR FRYING

1. Whisk all the ingredients, apart from the butter, together in a mixing bowl.

2. Heat a frying pan and melt a little butter. Pour in the mixture to form a pancake shape and top it with fruit.

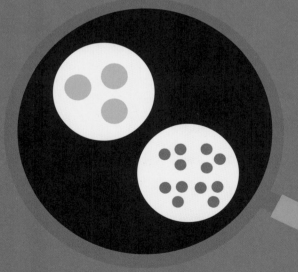

3. After two minutes, lift the edge with a spatula and check they are golden on the bottom. If they are, flip them over. They only need 30 seconds on the second side.

WARNING
Ask an adult to help with the cooking.

DAILY DARE

Got a 'yes' or 'no' decision only you can make? Try flipping a coin. If you are not happy with the result, you will know you wanted the other one!

Doodle some of the things about you that make you great!

DAILY DARE

Be curious. If you don't ask you really will never know. No one knows everything, so go ahead and ASK!

Write down some questions you want to know the answer to ... then go and find out the answers!

The wheel of feel!

How do you feel today? Find the word on the wheel!
Feelings can change a lot so do this on different days and try
writing or making art that shows how you feel.

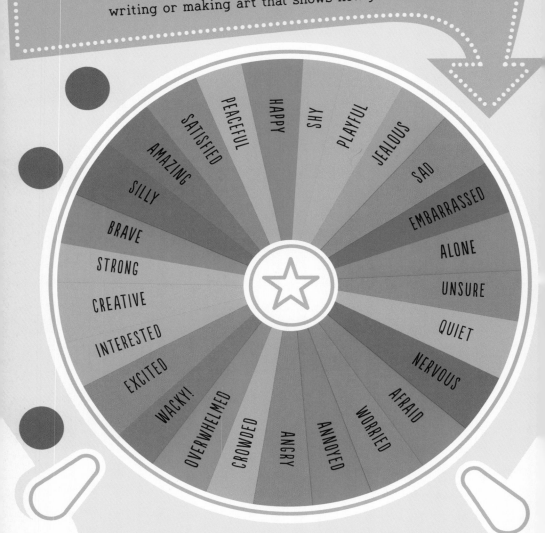

The wheel contains the following words:

SATISFIED, PEACEFUL, HAPPY, SHY, PLAYFUL, JEALOUS, SAD, EMBARRASSED, ALONE, UNSURE, QUIET, NERVOUS, AFRAID, WORRIED, ANNOYED, ANGRY, CROWDED, OVERWHELMED, WACKY!, EXCITED, INTERESTED, CREATIVE, STRONG, BRAVE, SILLY, AMAZING

'FEELING A LITTLE THIS BUT ALSO THAT'

These words won't always get it right. You can
have lots of feelings all at once so trying using
a few, and saying how much of each you feel.

New friends

It can be difficult making new friends,
but it gets easier with practice!

COMMON INTEREST

If you notice you
have a sport or
activity in common,
that's a great way to
get started.

BE PREPARED

If talking to new people makes you
nervous, think about things you
might say then practise talking and
asking questions at home.

TAKE A BREATHER

Give other people
time to answer or
respond.

ASK A QUESTION

Ask something! Maybe
something they're interested
in or that they're doing at
the time.

SMILE

If it feels right for you,
smiling can relax people
a bit. It just takes a bit of
practice when you're nervous.

USE YOUR SKILLS!

Maybe you have a good joke
you can tell, or are able to
join in with something you
already enjoy!

INTRODUCE YOURSELF

If you feel happy to, you
can tell them your name
and ask theirs.

Draw something or someone that inspires you.

DAILY DARE

Start a daily journal and always begin
with something positive about your day.

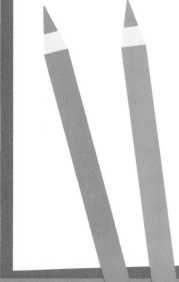

YOUR best life

Make yourself a card for every birthday you've ever had. Theme the design with the amazing thing you discovered that year.

AGE 1 ....Smiles and giggles....

AGE 2 ....

AGE 3 ....

AGE 4 ....

Look at photos or ask a family member what they remember, if you aren't sure.

AGE 5 ....

AGE 6 ....

AGE 7 ....

AGE 8 ....

AGE 9 ....

AGE 10 ....

Imagine what you'll learn in the future! Make
birthday cards with things you'd like to learn!

Lionheart

Be brave! Try something you've always been nervous of ...

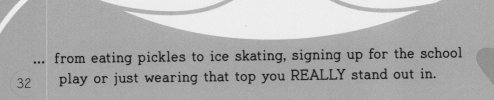

... from eating pickles to ice skating, signing up for the school play or just wearing that top you REALLY stand out in.

Impossible

If you think things are impossible and don't try, they will always be impossible! You don't know what's possible until you give things a try, so do it!

Can you copy this patch on to your bag or anywhere else? Think it's impossible? Then turn the page.

Challenge Impossible

Impossible patch

Everything is easier when you break it down.
For your own version of the impossible patch
design, use the instructions but don't worry
about being perfect! Make it your own.

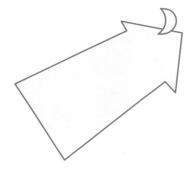

1. Draw the arrow and a
   moon. Start in pencil and
   draw over in pen when
   you're happy.

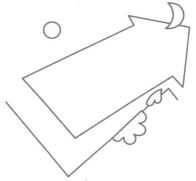

2. Add a floating circle.
   Draw the base of the
   arrow below it. Add
   small clouds.

3. Draw three connecting
   lines to create the 3D
   arrow. Add a large cloud.

4. Draw a big cloud
   around the base. Add
   the rainbow and star.

Possible

When you're finished, write whatever inspires you in the arrow. Use the bubble writing from page 18 if you like!

5. Colour in the base. You can do each section in different patterns. Draw in more clouds.

6. Keep adding more stars and clouds.

7. Add in more stars and colour in some blocked in areas. Use any colours.

8. Add in more squiggles and lines. You can do anything you like!

Speak up

Get heard above the crowd
with these 'pro' speech tips.

RUB IT IN

Press into your jaw lightly
and make little circles. This
little massage will loosen
your face right up!

FINISH LOW!

If you want to make a clear
point, end with a lower tone so
you sound sure! If your voice
goes up it will sound more like
a question.

E - NUN - CI - ATE

Say each part of the word very
sharply and cleanly. You can't go too
big on this! Challenge someone to
see who can say it fastest without
making any mistakes!

I scream, you scream, we all
scream for ice-cream.

The cat catchers can't catch
caught cats.

SPEAK FROM YOUR BELLY

Try saying, 'Hello my name is ... '. OK, now take a big, slow, deep breath into your belly. If you're doing it right, your shoulders will stay relaxed and your tummy will move in and out. Practise for a while until you get the hang of it. Now, on the breath out, try saying it again.

SMILE WHILE YOU TALK

People will hear your positivity, it even works on the phone!

MAKE A YAWN

Yawn and then let out a big sigh. Don't force it. Once you've started your yawn, you can just relax! This will open and relax your throat.

Strut!

Take a walk whilst listening to something that makes you feel energised and happy

HEAD
Hold it high.

WALK TALL

STEP
Take each step in time with the music.

ARMS
Swing them along.

STRIDE
Take long, confident steps.

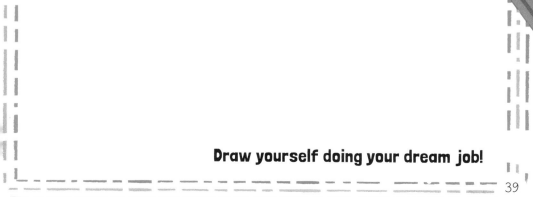

Draw yourself doing your dream job!

To-do list

So many things to do? Make a list.

Achieving goals no matter how small can feel good.
Tick each one off when you're done. Try adding
some fun stuff - that's important too.

Collect happy

Every time something happens that makes you happy, write it down in one of the circles below.

If you want to do this some more, just use an old jar and write each happy thought on a scrap of paper.

Loop the loop

Science says this is the coolest, calmest
thing you can doodle. Give it a go!

Going solo

Find stuff you love doing alone. Reading, music, playing solo ping-pong. It's important to know spending time with YOU is pretty great.

DAILY DARE

SPARK IT! Share something you love with others. It could be a game, a sport, baking, fashion and if people enjoy it you could even start your own club.

Draw something you're afraid of.
Then make it look seriously silly!

Friend zone

Friends can really do us good. Spend more time with the people who lift you up.

MAKES ME LAUGH

STUDY PAL

SUPER KIND

BASKETBALL BUD

LOVES ART TOO!

BEST LISTENER

COMIC BOOK BUD

OLD FRIEND

HOLIDAY PEN PAL

DANCE PARTNER

MATHS CLUB PAL

FAMILY FRIEND

If you notice you don't feel happy or relaxed with a particular person, it's OK to not spend too much time with them.

Just ask

Even if you don't think you need it today, practise asking for help with one of these things.

READING

PACKING

CLEANING YOUR ROOM

HELP WITH HOMEWORK

SHARING YOUR LUNCH

PLAYING A GAME

ARTS AND CRAFTS

My shop!

If you had a little shop what would you fill it with? Fill the boutique window with all the things that are unique and special about YOU!

Cat's curiosity

Curiosity didn't kill the cat, in fact it made her quite interesting and knowledgeable instead.

LISTEN
Listen carefully to exactly what people say, they'll appreciate it.

WAIT
Don't interrupt unless they talk for a very long time without a break!

THINK
Asking thoughtful questions shows that you are interested and were listening.

REMEMBER
No one knows everything, including experts. But if you don't ask, you'll never know!

HEADLINES

Read more than attention-grabbing headlines, they aren't facts!

DAILY DARE

Not 100% sure of the facts? Be a fact detective! Try this with any information you're told today!

LOOK FURTHER

Find out more about the subject. Use the internet and local library.

PRETTY PICTURES

Is there an infographic or graph? Look carefully at what is being shown, especially any words used. Does it all make sense?

SOURCE IT

Where is the information from? Is it trustworthy? Do other sources support it? Can you find other articles by the same person? What are these like?

KEYWORDS

Read each sentence carefully. Perhaps the sentence suggests something rather than states a fact.

Speak EASY!

If you sometimes think you can't do the things you would really like to, use these handy cup phones and get that brain chatter translated!

WHAT IF I DON'T LIKE IT?

WHAT IF I'M NOT GOOD AT IT?

BUT I'M AFRAID.

I CAN'T DO THAT.

I AM BAD AT THINGS.

I might be good at it! If I don't try I'll never ever know!

What if I enjoy it? If I don't try, I'll never know!

WHAT IF PEOPLE DON'T LIKE ME?

I am afraid but that's OK. Doing something you're nervous of takes courage and it's good to practise being brave

What if I make new friends?

Everyone starts on day one, even the best of the best. Getting good at anything takes practice and patience.

Even when things don't go right, I'm still learning! And you don't have to be the best to enjoy it.

Art, LIVE!

Take a camera or sketchbook and record the things you see out in public places.

You may draw attention to yourself but after a while you won't even notice.

POWER BALLAD

Singing can make you feel great.

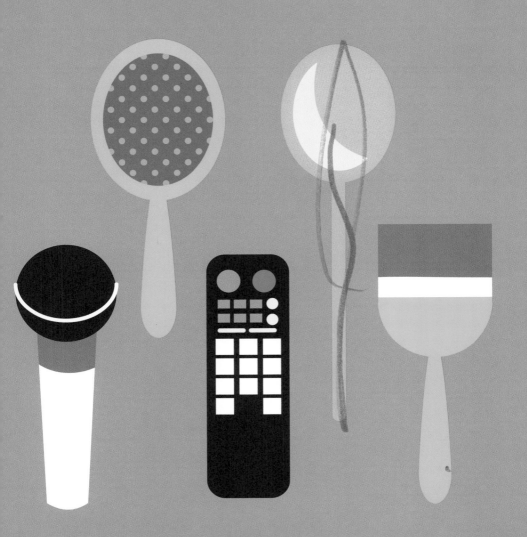

Choose an empowering song, find a pretend microphone, and sing it out! You can do this alone or have a karaoke party, so everyone can get a go!

Style and shine!

Wear what YOU love!

DO YOU FEEL
GOOD IN IT?

IS IT GOING TO BE OK
FOR WHAT YOU'RE DOING?

IN FASHION? WHO
CARES?

Try clashing
bold
patterns
and prints.

Customise and get creative!

Wearing bright or colourful colours and patterns can be nerve-racking as you might stand out - but bright colours can sometimes lift your mood, and the mood of those around you. If you love wearing black all over, and that makes you happy, that's great too!

Mix and match things you wouldn't usually try.

IS IT COMFORTABLE?

Draw yourself as a superhero! What magic powers would you have? What would you do with them?

Look up!

Take a day off from looking at digital devices! Write or draw the things you saw.

Flower power

Keeping a plant healthy can be very
satisfying. Choose something you like the
look of and research how to care for it.

SUNSHINE

All plants need some sun. Start
them in a sunny spot but if they
are not happy, they'll tell you.
Move them somewhere else!

SAY HELLO

Some people play music
and talk to their plants.
Try it if you want to!

WATER

Some plants need water more than others. To find out, identify your plant.
Most houseplants should dry out between watering - you can poke your finger
2 cm in the soil and, if it feels a little cold, wait before watering again. Cacti and
succulents only want water once in a while. Ferns should never have dry soil.
But remember: no plant should be sat in lots of water.

No problem!

Write about something that went wrong.
Then write three good things about it.

WHAT WENT WRONG?

How did you handle it?
Would you do it the same
way again?

Did you learn something?
If not yet, think!

Will you try it
again? Why?

Proud of you

Look back through the book. Draw or
write anything that boosted your
confidence ... then do more of that.

NOTES

NOTES

Heavy load

If you see anyone struggling with too many bags on your street, offer them a hand.

They'll be grateful for the offer, even if they say, 'no thanks!'

Kindness spotter

Look out for these little acts of kindness ...

FEEDING
THE BIRDS

CARING
FOR THE
OUTDOORS

OPENING
DOORS

SAYING,
'GOOD MORNING!'

SHARING

CHECKING IN

VOLUNTEERING

TEACHING OR
HELPING

Happy days

Think really hard about your day, and remember three things that you are grateful for.

Think! It might seem really small but a nice breakfast, a sunny day, a cool bug you saw or a person that made you laugh are all things to be thankful for!

A GOOD THING THAT HAPPENED TODAY IS ... IT MADE ME FEEL VERY ...

A PERSON THAT MADE ME SMILE TODAY IS ... BECAUSE THEY

TODAY I FELT LUCKY BECAUSE ...

I LAUGHED TODAY WHEN ...

TODAY I LEARNED ...

Hello pet

Dogs and (most!) cats love to show us some love. Here's how to love them back.

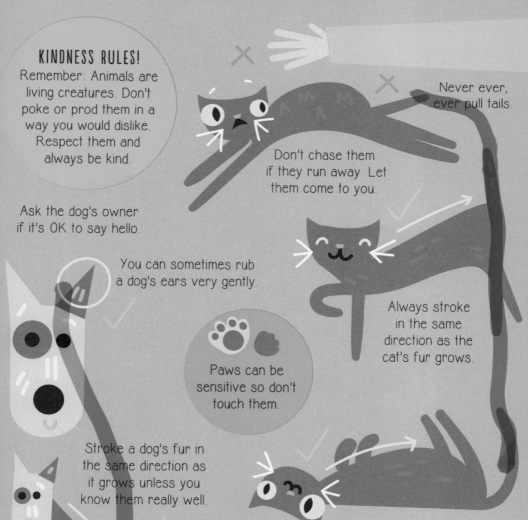

KINDNESS RULES!
Remember: Animals are living creatures. Don't poke or prod them in a way you would dislike. Respect them and always be kind.

Never ever, ever pull tails.

Don't chase them if they run away. Let them come to you.

Ask the dog's owner if it's OK to say hello.

You can sometimes rub a dog's ears very gently.

Paws can be sensitive so don't touch them.

Always stroke in the same direction as the cat's fur grows.

Stroke a dog's fur in the same direction as it grows unless you know them really well.

If a cat or dog shows their tummy, they might want a tummy stroke. Be very gentle when they do this. It is a big compliment as they are trusting you to be kind in this position.

Body brilliant

This poor skeleton has got nobody to tell him how brilliant they are. Can you help?

HAND

Write down a cool thing about each body part!

HEAD

ARM

CHEST

LEG

FOOT

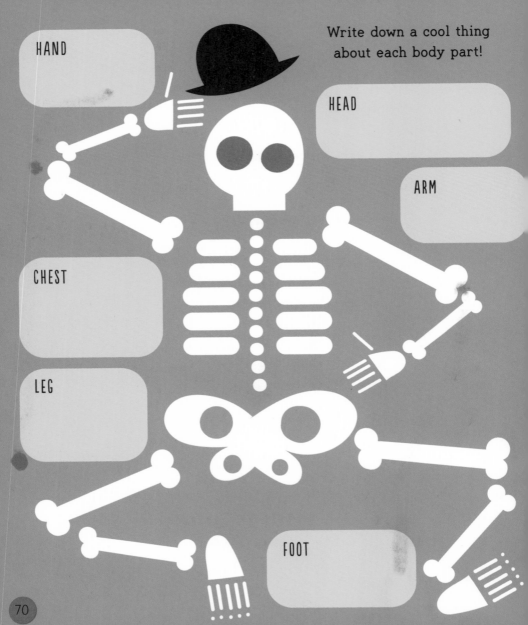

Design a themed cake for a charity bake
sale supporting a cause you care about.

Rainbow rememberer

Make a cheery rainbow bracelet for yourself, a friend or someone who you think might need a little help or some good cheer at the moment.

YOU WILL NEED
EMBROIDERY DARNING THREADS
SCISSORS TO TRIM
OPTIONAL BEADS

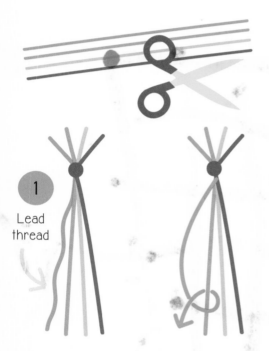

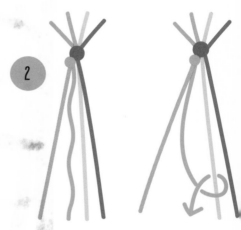

Lead thread

1

Start with four threads, each a different colour. Secure them together with a bead at the top. Spread the threads out. The thread on the left is your lead thread. Loop the lead thread around the thread beside it.

2

The lead thread stays the same. Loop the lead thread around the next thread. Make sure you tighten the loop all the way to the top knot, as shown above.

When it fits around your wrist, add a bead to the end ...

DAILY DARE

Have a cause or charity you'd like to support? Make a bracelet in the campaign colours! Don't forget to put some money in the charity box too.

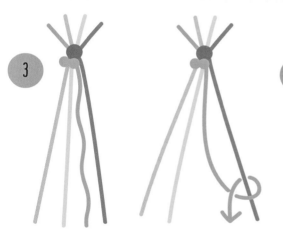

3

Repeat this looping action with the lead thread until you reach the last thread. The knots will have formed a little row at the top.

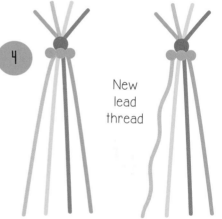

4

New lead thread

The thread on the left becomes the new lead thread. Repeat steps 1 to 3 until you have a full bracelet of little rows!

... and tie a knot to secure it! Et voilà! Jewellery!

Mirror mirror

Hold this book up in front of you in the mirror and read what it says.

FIRST CLASS
SMILE

YOU ARE
GORGEOUS

HELLO
WONDERFUL
YOU

YOU ARE
BRILLIANTLY
BRAVE

DAILY DARE

HUGS are powerful! Ask Mum or Nan or your auntie Paula, or your stepdad Paul (whoever it is) if you can give them a hug!

Hugs can make magic chemistry in our bodies happen and actually chill people out. That's some kind science!

Bugged out

Spied a spider? Help bugs get outside, there's no need to cause them any harm. Here's how to do it!

First, think! Spiders catch other bugs. Is a normal house spider really bothering you? If not, you can leave them be.

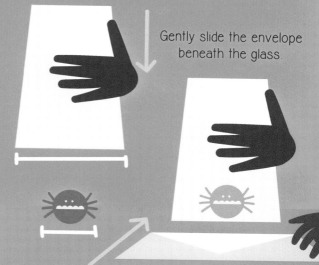

Gently slide the envelope beneath the glass.

Use a glass bigger than the spider to trap them. Be careful of delicate legs!

When the top is covered completely you can move them safely outside.

Open windows for flying bugs to escape in their own time. At night, don't leave lights on when windows are open. Bugs aren't too bright and are attracted to the lights, even though they'd much rather be outside.

WARNING If you live somewhere where these bugs are venomous or you have allergies, just ask for some help.

Art's eye view

Artists don't think people are ugly and actually prefer a more interesting face anyway!
Look at each part of your face in a mirror or photo and draw it in the labelled square.

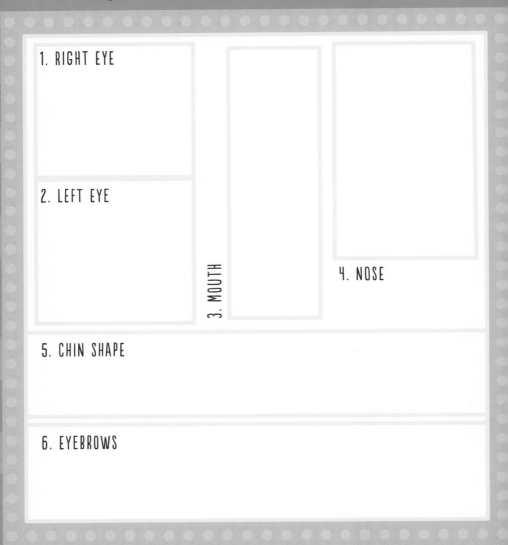

1. RIGHT EYE

2. LEFT EYE

3. MOUTH

4. NOSE

5. CHIN SHAPE

6. EYEBROWS

REMIX!

Copy each feature on to this page following the numbers to rearrange your face back to its usual set up! I tell you, it is a work of art.

6.

1.

4.

2.

3.

5.

Draw a kind, flattering picture of someone who you find a little annoying! You have to think hard about all their good bits to do this.

DAILY DARE

Yay you! Say something nice to a friend today.

You are funny!

I like your music taste.

Nice T-shirt!

Good shot!

You are my favourite person to see movies with.

You're really good at maths.

Chalk it up

Leave an inspiring chalk doodle or message outside your home. You can even draw out a hopscotch on the pavement for other kids to enjoy!

Throw a stone on to a number. Hop on to each number except where the stone lies. When you get to it, pick it up, continue to the end and then hop back to the start.

LOSE
RIGHT

When your team
is winning, show
them some love.

When they
are losing,
do it too!

Skill share

Share a skill you're good at with someone! You could help a sibling with homework or teach your pal a dance move.

Talk about how to do it, even the bits that seem obvious to you.

FIRST, SHOW THEM HOW TO DO IT.

Give some little tips.

Break it down, or do it slowly so they can see each stage.

NOW ... GIVE THEM A TURN!

Make their first
go a bit easier.

Tell them what they did
right and how they can
improve. Be kind, as
it can be easy to put
someone off.

Be patient!
Always remember
what's easy for you
is sometimes really
tough for others.

Pick it up

You don't want your walk to school or your park time to be total rubbish! Be kind to where you live and clean up mess … even if you didn't make it.

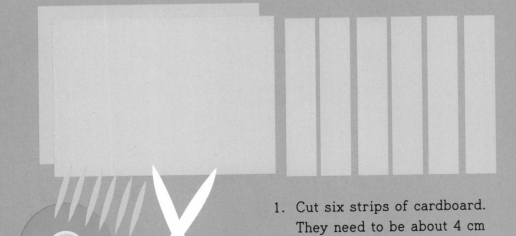

1. Cut six strips of cardboard. They need to be about 4 cm wide and 15 cm long.

2. Cut out two circles, both about 15 cm wide.

3. Cut one circle in half with a zigzag line and the other in half with a straight line.

WARNING
Use tools or wear gloves when picking up rubbish.

4. Use toothpicks to join two strips together in the middle to make three crosses.

5. Join the ends of the three crosses together with more toothpicks.

6. Use lots of duct tape around the ends of the picks so the sharp ends are well covered.

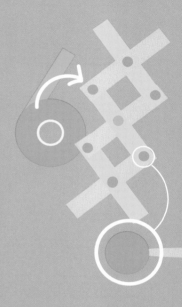

7. Use duct tape to reinforce your strips without taping them together.

8. Attach the semicircles to the ends as shown. They should be closest to their other halves.

Now let's get picking!

You time

Slow down and show yourself some kindness ...
you're the first person who knows you need it.

EXPLORE YOUR CLOSET

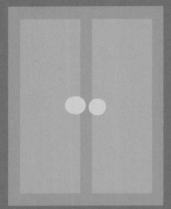

Look for unused toys or
games, or try on outfits.

JOURNAL

KNIT OR CRAFT

MAKE

DAYDREAM AND IMAGINE

COLLECT
LEAVES

READ WHATEVER YOU LIKE

LISTEN TO
MUSIC

DRAW OR COLOUR

BUG HUNT

NAP

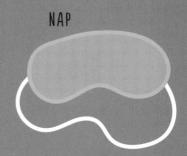

JUGGLE OR
HULA-HOOP

DAILY DARE

Smile, wave and make a funny face at little kids you pass in prams, on buses and stuck in traffic jams.

Babies and toddlers tend to stare first, so ... wait for it!

PLAY PEEK-A-BOO

BLOWING RASPBERRIES

WIDE SMILES

GAZING ABOUT

GOOFY GLASSES

Press the ends of your glasses to make them go up and down.

Thank you card

Take the time to tell someone how much you appreciate them! It can be something big or small, like one of the below!

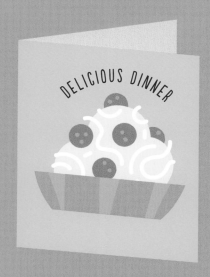

Stay cool

Grrrrrr! Sometimes we all get cross! It's good to say how you feel but if you can practise staying cool you won't get as upset and people can understand you more clearly. Try these top tips!

COUNT
Try slowly counting to 10.

CHILL
Step away and return when you feel calm.

RELAX
Lie down and, from head to toe, relax each body part so that it feels super heavy.

BREATHE
Take long slow breaths.

HEAD TO HEART
Can you hear your feelings or are there too many? Try writing them down.

PEACE
Have quiet time before you do anything you find tiring.

Kindness to robots

When you speak to voice-activated devices like Alexa or Google, use kind language!

Don't be rude or aggressive. Being kind is a practice, so do it whenever you can.

Create a kindness flag inspired by your favourite things.

It's in the post

Write a letter to someone you haven't seen in a while.
This simple act means SOOOO much to those who
will no doubt be missing (fabulous) you.

A kindness award

Create some awards and hand them out to the most worthy of winners. Here are some ideas!

FUNNIEST

BEST FRIEND

MOST KIND

MOST POSITIVE
PERSON

BEST
GIGGLE

TOP LISTENER

Kindness is back! Spread the word.

Design your own 'BE KIND' badge.

BELLY LAUGH

Making someone laugh is a kind thing to do.
Write your favourite joke inside the belly and jot
down everyone's names you tell it to in the bubble.

Magic hands

Our hands do pretty incredible things!
See how many of these things you do with your
hands in a single day! Can you think of any more?

EATING

DOING SPORTS

THUMBS UP

WRITING

TEXTING

FIST BUMP

HELLO AND GOODBYE

APPLAUSE

DRAWING

PLAYING CARDS

Just give

Donate something to charity.

Be kind and give things in good condition. Wash clothes or teddies first. It is a really nice thing to do.

You've got a big heart

Let's get moving and take care of our bodies!

Getting our heart to beat faster for about
one hour a day is incredibly body kind.

But don't do something
you don't like!

Try lots of different
activities until you find
the one you like.

Then doing it a lot will
be mind kind too!!

Draw a feel-good picture of someone you think is great!

Think!

Write down an act of kindness someone has shown you!
Fill one cloud for each person you can think of. Do
more in a notebook if there are more than four.

DAILY DARE

This one's easy. Share your crisps, your football or just your time! You can really make someone's day.

No thank you!

Being kind to yourself sometimes means saying no to people. This can be hard but being kind to yourself is really important.

HEAR YOUR VOICE
Write down your thoughts and feelings to help you un-jumble them if you aren't sure how you feel.

NO!
Someone not taking NO for an answer? You don't have to change your mind because someone doesn't accept it. In fact, it's important that you don't change your mind just because you feel pressured to.

MAYBE?
Not 100% sure but feel like you have to decide right now? It's always OK to say 'no thank you' first and then change your mind later. In fact, it's always OK to change your mind. It works the other way too.

YES?

NO?

SAY NO KINDLY

If you have a reason that is not to do with them, you can explain why you're saying no in a kind way. Being polite helps too, so just say 'not this time, but thank you for asking.'

VALUE YOU

Listen to your own head and heart. You are pretty great and you'll show that most when you feel safe, calm and happy.

TOTAL RESPECT!

Remember: it's OK for you to say 'no' and it's OK for others to do the same. Always accept no for an answer too.

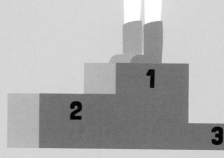

PERSONAL SPACE

It's always important that you feel safe with those around you. If you are ever worried, you should speak with a trusted adult.

Draw a memory of when someone was kind to you.

Head rest

Try these three quick, but super-weird, ways to chill yourself right out!

RAINDROPS

Lift your hands above your head and gently drum on your scalp with your fingertips.

RUB THOSE EARS

Use your thumbs and fingertips and rub your earlobes gently in circles. Close your eyes if it helps.

HAPPY PLACE

Use your fingertip and press gently on the space between your eyebrows. Now move your finger in circles while you press.

Sweet dreams

During sleep, your body and brain get some super TLC (tender love and care). Can you sleep for more than ten hours a night? Try these handy tips.

DAYTIME

EAT PLENTY OF HEALTHY FOOD

EXERCISE

GET OUTSIDE

RELAX

HAVE A NICE BATH

AVOID FIZZY DRINKS

NO SCREENS BEFORE BED

BRUSH YOUR TEETH

NIGHT-TIME

READ A
BOOK

PERFECT PLACE

Make sure your
bedroom is quiet
and dark.

PUT ON COMFY CLEAN NIGHT CLOTHES

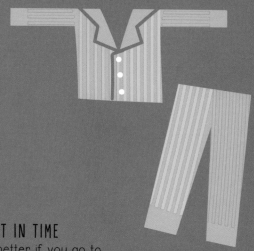

GET IN TIME

It works better if you go to
bed and wake at the same
time each time, so you might
need a few tries.

SWEET DREAMS

NO PETS ON THE BED

STOP!

Take a day or night to do a lot of whatever you like, but make sure it's not something that could be considered useful in any way!

DOODLE

DO AEROPLANES
(Arms out and spin!)

COLLECT GROOVY STONES

LOOK FOR BUGS

DAYDREAM

PUT YOUR FEET IN THE AIR!

CLOUD OR STARGAZE

ENJOY A SUNSET OR SUNRISE

A smile can make someone feel welcome!
Draw some big, kind smiles.

Create your own kindness monster! What features would they have? Think about what they need them for.

DAILY DARE

Here are some future good
deeds you can do today!

CHANGE IT UP
Find a penny, pick it up ...
put it in a charity box!

VOLUNTEER
Help support events and people
planning these positive events
by offering your time.

PAY IT FORWARD
Support local cafés who have
schemes to help the homeless.

PASS IT ON
Share your knowledge. You might
inspire someone to do good too!

Catnap

Have a quiet rest. You don't have to fall asleep, just shut your eyes and have ten minutes of quiet. If you have a pet to chill with, that's even better.

Positively you

Finish these sentences about yourself!
Everyone deserves to like themselves a whole lot because,
you know what, you're pretty great!

I LIKE TO ...

I AM GOOD AT ...

MY FAVOURITE COLOUR IS ...

BECAUSE ...

I AM FUNNY WHEN ...

MY FAVOURITE
BODY PART IS ...

you find thinking about your best bits tricky, ask people you love to help you out.

DAILY DARE

Just do one of these things without being asked at home. Sometimes the little things make someone's day!

RAKE LEAVES

MAKE A BED

SET OR TIDY AWAY
THE DINNER TABLE

WASH A CAR

WASH UP

TAKE OUT
THE RUBBISH

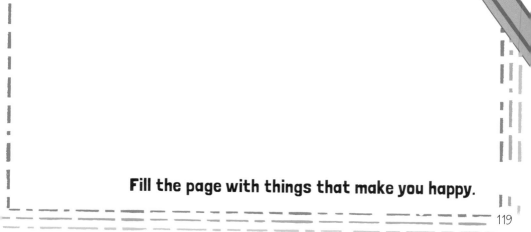

Fill the page with things that make you happy.

Cake for all!

Put smiles on faces! Bake these cupcakes, top with joyful decorations and share with friends and family.

You will need

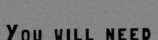

110 G BUTTER
110 G CASTER SUGAR
A PINCH OF SALT
110 G PLAIN FLOUR
2 TSP BAKING POWDER
2 MEDIUM EGGS
1 TSP VANILLA EXTRACT

To decorate:

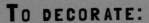

Add frosting or buttercream and then top with decorations like edible glitter! You'll find amazing toppings in most shops, just look in the baking aisle.

1. Place your paper cases into the muffin tray and turn the oven to 180°C (Gas mark 4).

2. Cut the butter into cubes and put into the warming oven for a few minutes, until it's a little softer, but not melted.

3. Put the butter into a mixing bowl with the sugar and beat into a smooth cream with a wooden spoon.

WARNING
Make sure you put on oven gloves when you use the oven.

4. Add a pinch of salt and sift the flour and baking powder into the bowl.

5. Use a fork to mix the eggs and vanilla together in a separate jug.

6. Pour the egg mixture into the mixing bowl and beat everything together with the wooden spoon.

7. When the mix is ready, use a tablespoon to scoop out some mix, then use another spoon to push it into the cake case.

8. Put the tray into the hot oven and cook for about 20 minutes. When the cakes are golden, put the muffin tray on to a cooling rack.

9. After ten minutes, remove them from the muffin tray to finish cooling on the rack.

THEN DECORATE!

Want to do even more? Take part in a bake sale for charity!

Memories

Look back on your journey of kindness.
Write down your favourite memories!

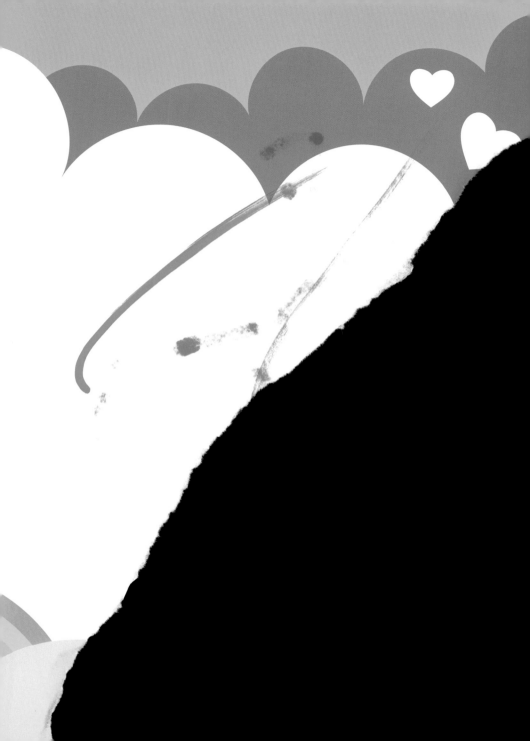

NOTES

NOTES

KINDNESS BADGES:
COLLECT ALL 6!

CREATURE KIND

RANDOM ACTS OF KINDNESS

Share the
JOY

Kindness for Friends

& Family

F&F

BODY
BRILLIANT

G
GOOD
TO ME
T   M

This book belongs to: (give yourself an awesome nickname)

....

COMPLETION SCORES

Select how confident you are now, out of 5.

Meeting new people: ★ ★ ★ ★ ★

Trying new things: ★ ★ ★ ★ ★

Asking for help: ★ ★ ★ ★ ★

Feeling good about me: ★ ★ ★ ★ ★

Speaking up: ★ ★ ★ ★ ★

Overall confidence level: ★ ★ ★ ★ ★

Time for kind

Now you have completed this book, you'll hopefully have found a few things that make you feel more confident and kind. So be brave, have courage and keeping making the world a better place for everyone.